C Programming Professional Made Easy

Sam Key

Expert C Programming Language Success In A Day For Any Computer User!

2nd Edition

Copyright 2015 by Sam Key - All rights reserved.

Table Of Contents

Introduction

I want to thank you and congratulate you for purchasing the book, *"Professional C Programming Made Easy: Expert C Programming Language Success In A Day For Any Computer User!"*.

This book contains proven steps and strategies on how to understand and perform C programming. C is one of the most basic programming tools used for a wide array of applications. Most people stay away from it because the language seem complicated, with all those characters, letters, sequences and special symbols.

This book will break down every element and explain in detail each language used in the C program. By the time you are done with this book, C programming language will be easy to understand and easy to execute.

Read on and learn.

Thanks again for purchasing this book. I hope you enjoy it!

Chapter 1 The Basic Elements Of C

The seemingly complicated C program is composed of the following basic elements:

Character Set

The alphabet in both upper and lower cases is used in C. The 0-9 digits are also used, including white spaces and some special characters. These are used in different combinations to form elements of a basic C program such as expressions, constants, variables, etc.

Special characters include the following:

> + ,. *– / % = & ! #?"^ '| / ( )< > { }[ ] ;: @ ~!

White spaces include:

- Blank space

- Carriage return

- Horizontal tab

- Form feed

- New line

Identifiers

An identifier is a name given to the various elements of the C program, such as arrays, variables and functions. These contain digits and letters in various arrangements. However, identifiers should always start with a letter. The letters may be in upper case, lower case or both. However, these are not interchangeable. C programming is case sensitive, as each letter in different cases is regarded as separate from each other. Underscores are also permitted because it is considered by the program as a kind of letter.

Examples of valid identifiers include the following:

`ab123`

`A`

`stud_name`

`average`

`velocity`

`TOTAL`

Identifiers need to start with a letter and should not contain illegal characters. Examples of invalid identifiers include the following:

2nd — should always start with a letter

"Jamshedpur" - contains the illegal character (")

stud name — contains a blank space, which is an illegal character

stud-name — contains an illegal character (-)

In C, a single identifier may be used to refer to a number of different entities within the same C program. For instance, an array and a variable can share one identifier. For example:

The variable is `int difference, average, A[5]; //`
`sum, average`

The identifier is `A[5]`.

In the same program, an array can be named **A**, too.

`__func__`

The `__func__` is a predefined identifier that provides
functions names and makes these accessible and ready for
use anytime in the function. The complier would
automatically declare the `__func__` immediately after
placing the opening brace when declaring the function
definitions. The compiler declares the predefined identifier
this way:

```
static const char __func__[] = "Alex";
```

`"Alex"` refers to a specific name of this particular function.

Take a look at this example:

```
#include <stdio.h>


void anna1(void)    {

        printf("%sn",__func__);

        return;

}
```

```
int main() {

        myfunc();

}
```

What will appear as an output will be `anna1`

Keywords

Reserved words in C that come with standard and predefined meanings are called keywords. The uses for these words are restricted to their predefined intended purpose. Keywords cannot be utilized as programmer-defined identifiers. In C, there are 32 keywords being used, which include the following:

auto	else
break	extern
char	enum
case	goto
continue	for
const	if
do	long
default	int
double	register
float	short

return	union
sizeof	switch
signed	void
switch	unsigned
typedef	while
struct	volatile

Data Types

There are different types of data values that are passed in C. Each of the types of data has different representations within the memory bank of the computer. These also have varying memory requirements. Data type modifiers/qualifiers are often used to augment the different types of data.

Supported data types in C include int, char, float, double, void, _Bool, _Complex, arrays, and constants.

int

Integer quantities are stored in this type of data. The data type *int* can store a collection of different values, starting from INT_MAX to INT_MIN. An in-header file, <limits h>, defines the range.

These int data types use type modifiers such as unsigned, signed, long, long long and short.

Short int means that they occupy memory space of only 2 bytes.

A long int uses 4 bytes of memory space.

Short unsigned int is a data type that uses 2 bytes of memory space and store positive values only, ranging from 0 to 65535.

Unsigned int requires memory space similar to that of short unsigned int. For regular and ordinary int, the bit at the leftmost portion is used for the integer's sign.

Long unsigned int uses 4 bytes of space. It stores all positive integers ranging from 0 to 4294967295.

An int data is automatically considered as signed.

Long long int data type uses 64 bits memory. This type may either be unsigned or signed. Signed long long data type can store values ranging from −9,223,372,036,854,775,808 to 9,223,372,036,854,775,807. Unsigned long long data type stores value range of 0 to 18,446,744,073,709,551,615.

char

Single characters such as those found in C program's character set are stored by this type of data. The char data type uses 1 byte in the computer's memory. Any value from C program's character set can be stored as char. Modifiers that can be used are either `unsigned` or `signed`.

A char would always use 1 byte in the computer's memory space, whether it is signed or unsigned. The difference is on the value range. Values that can be stored as unsigned char range from 0 to 255. Signed char stores values ranging from −128 to +127. By default, a char data type is considered unsigned.

For each of the char types, there is a corresponding integer interpretation. This makes each char a special short integer.

float

A float is a data type used in storing real numbers that have single precision. That is, precision denoted as having 6 more digits after a decimal point. Float data type uses 4 bytes memory space.

The modifier for this data type is `long`, which uses the same memory space as that of double data type.

double

The double data type is used for storing real numbers that have double precision. Memory space used is 8 bytes. Double data type uses `long` as a type modifier. This uses up memory storage space of 10 bytes.

void

Void data type is used for specifying empty sets, which do not contain any value. Hence, void data type also occupies no space (0 bytes) in the memory storage.

_Bool

This is a Boolean type of data. It is an unsigned type of integer. It stores only 2 values, which is 0 and 1. When using _Bool, include **<stdboolh>**.

_Complex

This is used for storing complex numbers. In C, three types of _Complex are used. There is the `float _Complex`, `double _Complex`, and `long double _Complex`. These are found in <complex h> file.

Arrays

This identifier is used in referring to the collection of data that share the same name and of the same type of data. For example, all integers or all characters that have the same name. Each of the data is represented by its own array element. The subscripts differentiate the arrays from each other.

Constants

Constants are identifiers used in C. The values of identifiers do not change anywhere within the program. Constants are declared this way:

```
const datatype varname = value
```

`const` is the keyword that denotes or declares the variable as the fixed value entity, i.e., the constant.

In C, there are 4 basic constants used. These include the integer constant, floating-point, character and string constants. Floating-point and integer types of constant do not contain any blank spaces or commas. Minus signs can be used, which denotes negative quantities.

Integer Constants

Integer constants are integer valued numbers consisting of sequence of digits. These can be written using 3 different number systems, namely, decimal, octal and hexadecimal.

Decimal system (base 10)

An integer constant written in the decimal system contains combinations of numbers ranging from 0 to 9. Decimal constants should start with any number other except 0. For example, a decimal constant is written in C as:

```
const int size =76
```

Octal (base 8)

Octal constants are any number combinations from 0 to 7. To identify octal constants, the first number should be 0. For example:

```
const int a= 043; const int b=0;
```

An octal constant is denoted in the binary form. Take the octal 0347. Each digit is represented as:

$$0347 = 011\ 100\ 111 = 3 * 8^2 + 4 * 8^1 + 7 * 8^0 = 231$$

```
--- --- ---
 3   4   7
```

Hexadecimal constant (base 16)

This type consists of any of the possible combinations of digits ranging from 0 to 9. This type also includes letters a to f, written in either lowercase or uppercase. To identify hexadecimal constants, these should start with 0X or 0X. For example:

```
const int c= 0x7FF;
```

For example, the hexadecimal number 0x2A5 is internally represented in bit patterns within C as:

```
0x2A5 = 0010 1010 0101 = 2 * 16² + 10
* 16¹ + 5 * 16⁰ = 677
       ----  ----  ----
         2    A     5
```

Wherein, 677 is the decimal equivalent of the hexadecimal number 0x2.

Prefixes for integer constants can either be long or unsigned. A long integer constant (long int) ends with a 1 of L, such as 67354L or 673541. The last portion of an unsigned long integer constant should either be ul or UL, such as 672893UL or 672893ul. For an unsigned long long integer constant, UL or ul should be at the last portion. An unsigned constant should end with U or u, such as 673400095u or 673400095U. Normal integer constants are written without any suffix, such as a simple 67458.

Floating Point Constant

This type of constant has a base 10 or base 16 and contains an exponent, a decimal point or both. For a floating point constant with a base 10 and a decimal point, the base is replaced by an E or e. For example, the constant $1.8 * 10^{-3}$ is written as 1.8e-3 or 1.8E-3.

For hexadecimal character constants and the exponent is in the binary form, the exponent is replaced by P or p. Take a look at this example:

This type of constant is often precision quantities. These occupy around 8 bytes of memory. Different add-ons are allowed in some C program versions, such as F for a single precision floating constant or L for a long floating point type of constant.

Character Constant

A sequence of characters, whether single or multiple ones, enclosed by apostrophes or single quotation marks is called a character constant. The character set in the computer determines the integer value equivalent to each character constant. Escape sequences may also be found within the sequence of a character constant.

Single character constants enclosed by apostrophes is internally considered as integers. For example, 'A' is a single character constant that has an integer value of 65. The corresponding integer value is also called the ASCII value. Because of the corresponding numerical value, single character constants can be used in calculations just like how integers are used. Also, these constants can also be used when comparing other types of character constants.

Prefixes used in character constants such as L, U or u are used for character literals. These are considered as wide types of character constants. Character literals with the prefix L are considered under the type wchar_t, which are defined as <stddef.h> under the header file. Character constants that use the prefix U or u are considered as type char16_t or char32_t. These are considered as unsigned types of characters and are defined under the header file as <uchar.h>.

Those that do not have the prefix L are considered a narrow or ordinary character constant. Those that have escape sequences or are composed of at least 2 characters are considered as multicharacter constants.

Escape sequences are a type of character constant used in expressing non-printing characters like carriage return or tab. This sequence always begins with a backward slash, followed by special characters. These sequences represent a single character in the C language even if they are composed of more than 1 character. Examples of some of the most common escape sequences, and their integer (ASCII) value, used in C include the following:

Character	Escape Sequence	ASCII Value
Backspace	\b	008
Bell	\a	007
Newline	\n	010
Null	\o	000
Carriage	\r	013
Horizontal tab	\t	009
Vertical tab	\v	011
Form feed	\f	012

String Literals

Multibyte characters that form a sequence are called string literals. Multibyte characters have bit representations that fit into 1 or more bytes. String literals are enclosed within double quotation marks, for example, "A" and "Anna". There are 2 types of string literals, namely, UTF-8 string literals and wide string literals. Prefixes used for wide string literals include u, U or L. Prefix for UTF-8 string literals is u8.

Additional characters or extended character sets included in string literals are recognized and supported by the compiler. These additional characters can be used meaningfully to further enhance character constants and string literals.

Symbolic constants

Symbolic constants are substitute names for numeric, string or character constants within a program. The compiler would replace the symbolic constants with its actual value once the program is run.

At the beginning of the program, the symbolic constant is defined with a **# define** feature. This feature is called the preprocessor directive.

The definition of a symbolic constant does not end with a semi colon, like other C statements. Take a look at this example:

```
#define  PI  3.1415
```

(//PI is the constant that will represent value 3.1415)

```
#define  True 1
```

```
#define  name  "Alice"
```

For all numeric constants such as floating point and integer, non-numeric characters and blank spaces are not included. These constants are also limited by minimum and maximum bounds, which are usually dependent on the computer.

Variables

Memory locations where data is stored are called variables. These are indicated by a unique identifier. Names for variables are symbolic representations that refer to a particular memory location. Examples are *count, car_no* and *sum*.

Rules when writing the variable names

Writing variable names follow certain rules in order to make sure that data is stored properly and retrieved efficiently.

- Letters (in both lowercase and uppercase), underscore ('_') and digits are the only characters that can be used for variable names.

- Variables should begin either with an underscore or a letter. Starting with an underscore is acceptable, but is not highly recommended. Underscores at the beginning of variables can come in conflict with system names and the compiler may protest.

- There is no limit on the length of variables. The compiler can distinguish the first 31 characters of a variable. This means that individual variables should have different sequences for the 1st 31 characters.

Variables should also be declared at the beginning of a program before it can be used.

Chapter 2 What is C Programming Language?

In C, the programming language is a language that focuses on the structure. It was developed in 1972, at Bell Laboratories, by Dennis Ritchie. The features of the language were derived from "B", which is an earlier programming language and formally known as BCPL or Basic Combined Programming Language. The C programming language was originally developed to implement the UNIX operating system.

Standards of C Programming Language

In 1989, the American National Standards Institute developed the 1st standard specifications. This pioneering standard specification was referred to as C89 and C90, both referring to the same programming language.

In 1999, a revision was made in the programming language. The revised standard was called C99. It had new features such as advanced data types. It also had a few changes, which gave rise to more applications.

The C11 standard was developed, which added new features to the programming language for C. This had a library-like generic macro type, enhanced Unicode support, anonymous structures, multi-threading, bounds-checked functions and atomic structures. It had improved compatibility with C++. Some parts of the C99 library in C11 were made optional.

The Embedded C programming language included a few features that were not part of C. These included the named address spaces, basic I/O hardware addressing and fixed point arithmetic.

C Programming Language Features

There are a lot of features of the programming language, which include the following:

- Modularity

- Interactivity

- Portability

- Reliability

- Effectiveness

- Efficiency

- Flexibility

Uses of the C Programming Language

This language has found several applications. It is now used for the development of system applications, which form a huge portion of operating systems such as Linux, Windows and UNIX.

Some of the applications of C language include the following:

- Spreadsheets

- Database systems

- Word processors

- Graphics packages

- Network drivers

- Compilers and Assemblers

- Operating system development

- Interpreters

Chapter 3 Understanding C Program

The C program has several features and steps in order for an output or function is carried out.

Basic Commands (for writing basic C Program)

The basic syntax and commands used in writing a simple C program include the following:

```
#include <stdio.h>
```

This command is a preprocessor. <stdio.h> stands for standard input output header file. This is a file from the C library, which is included before the C program is compiled.

```
int main()
```

Execution of all C program begins with this main function.

```
{
```

This symbol is used to indicate the start of the main function.

```
}
```

This indicates the conclusion of the main function.

```
/* */
```

Anything written in between this command will not be considered for execution and compilation.

```
printf (output);
```

The printf command prints the output on the screen.

```
getch();
```

Writing this command would allow the system to wait for any keyboard character input.

```
return 0
```

Writing this command will terminate the C program or main function and return to 0.

A basic C Program would look like this:

```
#include <stdio.h>
int main()
{
/* Our first simple C basic program */
printf("Hello People! ");
getch();
return 0;
}
```

The output of this simple program would look like this:

```
Hello People!
```

Chapter 4 Learn C Programming

After learning the basic elements and what the language is all about, time to start programming in C. Here are the most important steps:

Download a compiler

A compiler is a program needed to compile the C code. It interprets the written codes and translates it into specific signals, which can be understood by the computer. Usually, compiler programs are free. There are different compilers available for several operating systems. Microsoft Visual Studio and MinGW are compilers available for Windows operating systems. XCode is among the best compilers for Mac. Among the most widely used C compiler options for Linux is gcc.

Basic Codes

Consider the following example of a simple C program in the previous chapter:

```
#include <stdio.h>


int main()

{

    printf("Hello People!\n");

    getchar();
```

```
    return 0;

}
```

At the start of the program, `#include` command is placed. This is important in order to load the libraries where the needed functions are located.

The `<stdio.h>` refers to the file library and allows for the use of the succeeding functions `getchar()` and `printf()`.

The command `int main ()` sends a message to the compiler to run the function with the name "main" and return a certain integer once it is done running. Every C program executes a main function.

The symbol `{ }` is used to specify that everything within it is a component of the "main" function that the compiler should run.

The function `printf()` tells the system to display the words or characters within the parenthesis onto the computer screen. The quotation marks make certain that the C compiler would print the words or characters as it is. The sequence `\n` informs the C compiler to place its cursor to the succeeding line. At the conclusion of the line, a `;` (semicolon) is placed to denote that the sequence is done. Most codes in C program needs a semicolon to denote where the line ends.

The command `getchar()` informs the compiler to stop once it reaches the end of the function and standby for an input from the keyboard before continuing. This command is very useful because most compilers would run the C program and then immediately exits the window. The `getchar()`

command would prevent the compiler to close the window until after a keystroke .is made.

The command `return 0` denotes that the function has ended. For this particular C program, it started as an `int`, which indicates that the program has to return an integer once it is done running. The "0" is an indication that the compiler ran the program correctly. If another number is returned at the end of the program, it means that there was an error somewhere in the program.

Compiling the program

To compile the program, type the code into the program's code editor. Save this as a type of *.c file, then click the Run or Build button.

Commenting on the code

Any comments placed on codes are not compiled. These allow the user to give details on what happens in the function. Comments are good reminders on what the code is all about and for what. Comments also help other developers to understand what the code when they look at it.

To make a comment, add a `/*` at the beginning of the comment. End the written comment with a `*/`. When commenting, comment on everything except the basic portions of the code, where explanations are no longer necessary because the meanings are already clearly understood.

Also, comments can be utilized for quick removal of code parts without having to delete them. Just enclose portions of the code in `/* */`, then compile. Remove these tags if these portions are to be added back into the code.

USING VARIABLES

Understanding variables

Define the variables before using them. Some common ones include `char`, `float` and `int`.

Declaring variables

Again, variables have to be declared before the program can use them. To declare, enter data type and then the name of the variable. Take a look at these examples:

```
char name;

float x;

int f, g, i, j;
```

Multiple variables can also be declared all on a single line, on condition that all of them belong to the same data type. Just separate the names of the variables commas (i.e., `int f, g, i, j;`).

When declaring variables, always end the line with a semicolon to denote that the line has ended.

Location on declaring the variables

Declaring variables is done at the start of the code block. This is the portion of the code enclosed by the brackets `{}`. The program won't function well if variables are declared later within the code block.

Variables for storing user input

Simple programs can be written using variables. These programs will store inputs of the user. Simple programs will use the function scanf, which searches the user's input for particular values. Take a look at this example:

```
#include <stdio.h>

int main()
{
    int x;

    printf( "45: " );
    scanf( "%d", &x );
    printf( "45 %d", x );
    getchar();
    return 0;
}
```

The string &d informs the function scanf to search the input for any integers.

The command & placed before the x variable informs the function scanf where it can search for the specific variable so that the function can change it. It also informs the function to store the defined integer within the variable.

The last `printf` tells the compiler to read back the integer input into the screen as a feedback for the user to check.

Manipulating variables

Mathematical expressions can be used, which allow users to manipulate stored variables. When using mathematical expressions, it is most important to remember to use the "=" distinction. A single = will set the variable's value. A == (double equal sign) is placed when the goal is to compare the values on both sides of the sign, to check if the values are equal.

For example:

```
x = 2 * 4; /* sets the value of "x" to 2 *
4, or 8 */

x = x + 8; /* adds 8 to the original "x "
value, and defines the new "x" value as the
specific variable */

x == 18; /* determines if the value of "x"
is equal to 18 */

x < 11; /* determines if the "x" value is
lower than 11 */
```

CONDITIONAL STATEMENTS

Conditional statements can also be used within the C program. In fact, most programs are driven by these statements. These are determined as either False or True and then acted upon depending on the results. The most widely used and basic conditional statement is `if`.

In C, False and True statements are treated differently. Statements that are "TRUE" are those that end up equal to nonzero numbers. For example, when a comparison is performed, the outcome is a "TRUE" statement if the returned numerical value is "1". The result is a "FALSE" statement if the value that returns is "0".

Basic conditional operators

The operation of conditional statements is based on mathematical operators used in comparing values. The most common conditional operators include the following:

< /* less than */

`6 < 15 TRUE`

> /* greater than */

`10 > 5 TRUE`

<= /* less than or equal to */

`4 <= 8 TRUE`

>= /* greater than or equal to */

`8 >= 8 TRUE`

!= /* not equal to */

`4 != 5 TRUE`

== /* equal to */

```
7 == 7 TRUE
```

How to write a basic "IF" conditional statement

A conditional "IF" statement is used in determining what the next step in the program is after evaluation of the statement. These can be combined with other types of conditional statements in order to create multiple and powerful options.

Take a look at this example:

```c
#include <stdio.h>


int main()

{

    if ( 4 < 7 )

        printf( "4 is less than 7");

        getchar();

}
```

The "ELSE/ELSE IF" statements

These statements can be used in expanding the conditional statements. Build upon the "IF" statements with "ELSE" and "ELSE IF" type of conditional statements, which will handle different types of results. An "ELSE" statement will be run when the IF statement result is FALSE. An "ELSE IF" statement will allow for the inclusion of multiple IF statements in one code block, which will handle all the various cases of the statement.

Take a look at this example:

```
#include <stdio.h>


int main()
{
  int age;


  printf( "Please type current age: " );

  scanf( "%d", &age );

  if ( age <= 10 ) {

    printf( "You are just a kid!\n" );

  }

  else if ( age < 30 ) {

    printf( "Being  a  young  adult  is
pretty awesome!\n" );

  }

  else if ( age < 50 ) {
```

```
        printf( "You are young at heart!\n"
);

    }

    else {

        printf( "Age comes with wisdom.\n" );

    }

    return 0;

}
```

The above program will take all the input from the user and will run it through the different defined IF statements. If the input (number) satisfies the 1st IF statement, the 1st `printf` statement will be returned. If it does not, then input will be run through each of the "ELSE IF" statements until a match is found. If after all the "ELSE IF" statements have been run and nothing works, the input will be run through the "ELSE" statement at the last part of the program.

LOOPS

Loops are among the most important parts of C programming. These allow the user to repeat code blocks until particular conditions have been met. Loops make implementing repeated actions easy and reduce the need to write new conditional statements each time.

There are 3 main types of loops in C programming. These are FOR, WHILE and Do... WHILE.

"FOR" Loop

The "FOR" loop is the most useful and commonly used type of loop in C programming. This loop continues to run the function until the conditions set for this loop are met. There are 3 conditions required by the FOR loop. These include initialization of the variable, meeting the condition and how updating of the variable is done. All of these conditions need not be met at the same time, but a blank space with semicolon is still needed to prevent the loop from running continuously.

Take a look at this example:

```
#include <stdio.h>

int main()
{
    int y;

    for ( y = 0; y < 10; y++;) {
        printf( "%d\n", y );
    }
    getchar();
}
```

The value of y has been set to 0, and the loop is programmed to continue running as long as the y value remains less than 10. At each run (loop), the y value is increased by 1 before the loop is repeated. Hence, once the value of y is equivalent to 10 (after 10 loops), the above loop will then break.

WHILE Loop

These are simpler than the FOR loops. There is only one condition, which is that as long as the condition remains TRUE, the loop continues to run. Variables need not to be initialized or updated, but can be done within the loop's main body.

Take a look at this example:

```c
#include <stdio.h>

int main()
{
    int y;

    while ( y <= 20 ){
        printf( "%d\n", y );
        y++;
    }
    getchar();
```

```
}
```

In the above program, the command y++ will add 1 to the variable *y* for each execution of the loop. When the value of *y* reaches 21, the loop will break.

DO...WHILE Loop

This is a very useful loop to ensure at least 1 run. FOR and WHILE loops check the conditions at the start of the loop, which ensures that it could not immediately pass and fail. DO...WHILE loops will check the conditions when the loop is finished. This ensures that the loop will run at last once before a pass and fail occurs.

Take a look at this example:

```c
#include <stdio.h>

int main()
{
    int y;

    y = 10;
    do {
        printf("This loop is running!\n");
    } while ( y != 10 );
```

```
getchar();

}
```

This type of loop displays the message whether the condition results turn out TRUE or FALSE. The y variable is set to 10. The WHILE loop has been set to run when the y value is not equal to 10, at which the loop ends. The message was printed because the condition is not checked until the loop has ended.

The WHILE portion of the DO..WHILE loop must end with a semicolon. This is also the only instance when a loop ends this way.

Chapter 5 Storage Classes

Storage class refers to the lifetime and visibility of functions and variables within a C program. Such specifiers are found before the type they modify. Some of the most commonly used storage classes in a C program include auto, static, register, and extern. So how are these storage classes used?

Auto

This storage class is considered as the default storage class for all the local variables. Consider this example:

```
{

int mount;

auto int month;

}
```

The above example has variables with a similar storage class. Take note that auto may only be used inside functions, such as local variables.

Register

This storage class is typically used for local variables that have to be stored inside a register instead of a RAM. The variable should have a size that is less than or equal to the size of the register. It should also not use the unary '&' operator because it does not include a memory. Look at this example:

```
{

register int kilometers;

}
```

Keep in mind that the register storage class will only be functional if used with variables that use quick access like counters. Also, you should take note that this storage class does not necessarily store the variable inside a register. Instead, it offers the possibility of storing that variable inside a register based on certain implementations of restrictions and hardware.

Static

This storage class commands the compiler to save a local variable throughout the lifetime of the program rather than destroying and creating it whenever it comes in and out of range. Turning your local variables into static allows them to retain their values amid function calls.

In addition, you can use the static modifier for global variables. If you do this, the scope of the variable can be regulated in the file in which it has been declared. Remember that if you use static on a member of the class data, all its class objects can share just one copy of its member.

```c
#include <stdio.h>
/* function declaration */
void func(void);
static int count = 5; /* global variable */
main()
{
while(count--)
{
func();
}
return 0;
}
/* function definition */
void func( void )
{
static int i = 5; /* local static variable */
i++;
printf("i is %d and count is %d\n", i, count);
}
```

The above sample program containing the storage class static yields the following result:

```
i is 6 and count is 4
i is 7 and count is 3
i is 8 and count is 2
i is 9 and count is 1
```

i is 10 and count is 0

Extern

This storage class is used to provide a global variable reference that can be seen in all program files. So whenever you use extern, you cannot initialize the variable because all it can do is point the name of the variable towards a specific storage location in which it has been defined before.

If you have several files but you want to define a global function or variable that you intend to use in your other files as well, you can use extern to provide a function or variable reference. You should keep in mind that extern is for declaring a global function or variable in another file. If there are several files that share similar global functions or variables, the extern modifier is used. Consider this example:

First File: main.c

```
#include <stdio.h>
int count ;
extern void write_extern();
main()
{
write_extern();
}
```

Second File: write.c

```
#include <stdio.h>
```

```
extern int count;
void write_extern(void)
{
count = 5;
printf("count is %d\n", count);
}
```

In this example, extern is defined in the first file and is used to declare count in the second file. If you compile both files as

```
$gcc main.c write.c
```

You can have the results of 5

Chapter 6 Operators

Operators are symbols that tell you to perform certain logical or mathematical manipulations. In the C language, there are plenty of built-in operators such as arithmetic, relational, logical, bitwise, assignment, and misc.

Arithmetic Operators

Let A = 10 and B = 20.

Operator	Description	Example
+	It adds two operands.	A + B = 30
-	It subtracts the second operand from the first operand.	A – B = -10
*	It multiplies the operands.	A * B = 200
/	It divides the numerator by the	B / A = 2

denominator.

%   It is a modulus operator. It gives the

$B \% A = 0$

remainder after an integer division.

++   It is an increments operator. It

$A++ = 11$

increases the value of the integer

by one.

--   It is a decrements operator. It   A--

$= 9$

decreases the value of the integer

by one.

Relational Operators

Let A = 10 and B =20.

Operator	Description	Example
==	It checks whether or not the values of both operands are equal. If they are equal, then the	(A == B) is not true.

	condition is true.	
!=	It checks whether or not the values of both operands are equal. If they are not equal, then the condition is true.	(A != B) is true.
>	It checks whether or not the value of the left operand is bigger than the value of the right operand. If it is, then the condition is true.	(A > B) is not true.
<	It checks whether or not the value of the left operand is less than the value of the right operand. If it is, then the condition is true.	(A < B) is true.
>=	It checks whether or not the value of the left operand is bigger than the value of the right operand. If it is, then the condition	(A >= B) is not true.

	is true.	
<=	It checks whether or not the value of the left operand is less than or equal to the value of the right operand. If it is, then the condition is true.	(A <= B) is true.

Logical Operators

Let A = 1 and B = 0.

Operator	Description	Example
&&	It is known as the Logical AND Operator. If the operands are non-zero, the condition is true. Otherwise, it is false.	(A && B) is false.
||	It is known as the Logical OR Operator. If one of the two operands is non-zero, the	(A || B) is true.

	condition is true.	
!	It is known as the Logical NOT Operator. It is used to reverse the logical state of the operand. If the condition is true, the Logical NOT Operator will make it false.	!(A && B) is true.

Bitwise Operators

These operators work on bits and perform bit-by-bit operation. This is the Truth Table for |, ^, and &.

p	q	p & q	p | q	p ^ q
0	0	0	0	0
0	1	0	1	1
1	1	1	1	0
1	0	0	1	1

If A = 6 and B = 13:

A = 00111100

B = 00001101

A & B = 00001100

47

A | B = 00111101

A ^ B = 00110001

~A = 11000011

Let A = 60 and B = 13.

Operator	Description	Example
&	It is known as the Binary AND Operator. It copies a bit if it exists in both operands.	(A & B) = 12, which is equivalent to 00001100 in binary.
		It is known as the Binary OR Operator. It copies a bit if it exists in either one of the operands.	(A | B) = 61, which is equivalent to 00111101 in binary.
^	It is known as the Binary XOR Operator. It copies a bit if it exists in just one operand.	(A ^ B) = 49, which is equivalent to 00110001 in binary.
~	It is known as the Binary Ones Complement	(~A) = -60, which is equivalent to 11000011 in

	Operator. It is unary and has the flipping bits effect.	binary.
<<	It is known as the Binary Left Shift Operator. The value of the left operand is moved to the left depending on how many	A << 2 = 240, which is equivalent to 11110000 in binary. bits the right operand specified.
>>	It is known as the Binary Right Shift Operator. The value of the left operand is moved to the right depending on how many bits the right operand specified.	A >> 2 = 15, which is equivalent to 00001111 in binary.

Assignment Operators

Operator	Description	Example
=	It is an assignment operator. It allocates values from the right operand to the left	C = A + B assigns the value of A + B into C.

49

	operand.	
+=	It is known as the add AND assignment operator. It adds the right operand to the left operand and then assigns the value to the left operand.	C += A is equal to C = C + A
-=	It is known as the subtract AND assignment operator. It subtracts the right operand from the left operand and then assigns the value to the left operand.	C -= A is equal to C = C – A
*=	It is known as the multiply AND assignment operator. It multiplies the right operand with the left operand and then assigns the value to the left operand.	C *= A is equal to C = C * A

/=	It is known as the divide AND assignment operator. It divides the left operand with the right operand and then assigns the result to the left operand.	C /= A is equal to C = C/A
%=	It is known as the modulus AND assignment operator. It takes modulus using two operands and assigns the result to the left operand.	C %= A is equal to C = C % A
<<=	It is known as the left shift AND assignment operator	C <<= 2 is equal to C = C << 2
>>=	It is known as the right shift AND assignment operator.	C >>= 2 is equal to C = C >> 2
&=	It is known as the bitwise AND assignment operator.	C &= 2 is equal to C & 2

^=	It is known as the bitwise exclusive OR and assignment operator.	C ^= 2 is equal to C ^ 2
|=	It is known as the bitwise inclusive OR and assignment operator.	C |= 2 is equal to C | 2

Chapter 7 Decision Making

The structures for decision making require you to specify at least one condition to be tested or evaluated by the program, along with statements that have to be executed if the condition is found to be true. However, statements that were found to be false can also be executed optionally. The general form of a decision making structure in most programming languages looks something like the example given below:

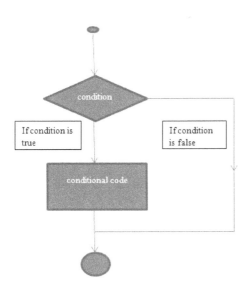

The C programming language assumes all non-null and non-zero values to be true. If there is either a null or zero, C assumes it to be false. The C programming language also makes use of the following decision making statements:

The If Statement

An if statement consists of a Boolean expression that is followed by at least one more statement.

Syntax

The syntax of an if statement is generally:

If (Boolean expression)

{

/* the statement(s) to be executed if the Boolean expression is true

*/

}

If the Boolean expression is found to be true, then the code inside the if statement is executed. Otherwise, the first set of code at the end of the if statement is executed.

As mentioned earlier, the C programming language assumes all non-null and non-zero values to be true while it assumes all null or zero values to be false.

Flow Diagram

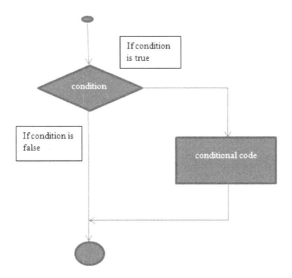

Example:

```
#include <stdio.h>
int main ( )
{
```

```
/* local variable definition */

int a = 10;

/* use the if statement to check the Boolean condition */

if ( a < 20 )

{

/* if the condition is true, the following should be printed */

printf ( "a is less than 20\n" );

}

printf ( "the value of a is : %d\n", a );

return 0;

}
```

Once the above code has been executed, it shows the following output:

a is less than 20;

the value of a is : 10

The If Else Statement

An if statement can be followed by an else state, which is optional. If the Boolean expression is false, then this statement is executed.

Syntax

The syntax of an if else statement is as follows:

if (Boolean expression)

{

/* the statement(s) to be executed if the Boolean expression is true */

}

else

{

/* the statement(s) to be executed if the Boolean expression is false */

}

If the Boolean expression is found to be true, then the if code is executed. On the other hand, if the Boolean expression is found to be false, then the else code is executed.

Again, the C programming language assumes all non-null and non-zero values to be true while it assumes all null or zero values to be false.

Flow Diagram

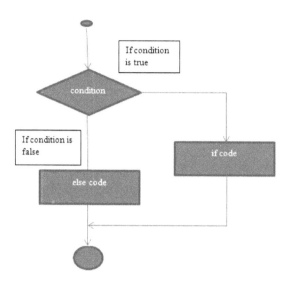

Example:

#include <stdio.h>

int main ( )

{

/* local variable definition */

int a = 100;

/* checking of the Boolean condition */

if (a < 20)

{

```
/* if the condition is true, the following should be printed */
printf ( "a is less than 20\n" );
}
else
{
/* if the condition is false, the following should be printed */
printf ( "a is not less than 20\n" );
}
printf ( "the value of a is : %d\n", a );
return 0;
}
```

Once the above code is executed, the following output is shown:

a is not less than 20;

the value of a is : 100

The If, Else If, Else Statement

An if statement can be followed by an else if, else statement, which is optional. This statement is highly useful for testing different conditions using the single if else statement. Then again, when using the if, else if, else statements, you should keep in mind the following pointers:

1. An if can have zero or more else if's. They have to come before the else.

2. An if can have zero or one else. It has to come after the else if.

3. If an else if is successfully executed, the remaining else's or else if's will no longer be tested.

Syntax

The general syntax of an if, else if, else statement is as follows:

if (first Boolean expression)

{

/* executes when the first Boolean expression is true */

}

else if (second Boolean expression)

{

/* executes when the second Boolean expression is true */

}

else if (third Boolean expression)

```
{
/* executes when the third Boolean expression is true */
}
else
{
/* executes when none of the above conditions is true */
}
```

Example:

```
#include <stdio.h>
int main ( )
{
/* local variable definition */
int a = 100;
/* checking of the Boolean condition */
if ( a == 10 )
{
/* if the condition is true, the following should be printed */
printf ("the value of a is 10\n" );
```

```
}
else if ( a == 20 )
{
/* if the else if condition is true, the following should be printed */
printf ("the value of a is 20\n" );
}
else if ( a == 30 )
{
/* if the else if condition is true */
printf ("the value of a is 30\n" );
}
else
{
/* if none of the above conditions is true */
printf ("None of the values match\n" );
}
printf ("The exact value of a is: %d\n", a );
return 0;
```

```
}
```

Once the above code is executed, the following output is shown:

None of the values match

The exact value of a is: 100

Nested If Statements

In the C programming language, you can test nest if else statements. This means that you can use one else if or if statement inside another else if or if statement(s).

Syntax

The general syntax for a nested if statement is as follows:

if (first Boolean expression)

{

/* executes when the first Boolean expression is true */

if (second Boolean expression)

{

/* executes when the second Boolean expression is true */

```
}

}


Example:

#include <stdio.h>

int main ( )

{

/* local variable definition */

int a = 100;

int b = 200;

/* checking of the Boolean condition */

if ( a == 100 )

{

/* if the condition is true, the following should be checked */

if ( b == 200 )

{

/* if the condition is true, the following should be printed */

printf ("The value of a is 100 and the value of b is 200\n" );

}
```

}

printf ("The exact value of a is : %d\n", a);

printf ("The exact value of b is: %d\n", b);

return 0;

}

Once the above code is executed, the following output is shown:

The value of a is 100 and the value of b is 200

The exact value of a is : 100

The exact value of b is : 200

Switch Statement

A switch statement allows a variable to undergo testing for equality against a list of values. Each one of the values is known as a case, and the variable being switched on is checked for every switch case.

Syntax

This is the general syntax for a switch statement:

switch (expression)

```
{

case constant-expression :

statement(s);

break;

/* optional */

case constant-expression :

statement(s);

break;

/* optional */

/* any number of case statements can be used */

default :

/* optional */

statement(s);

}
```

The following rules should be applied to a switch statement:

1. The case labels should be unique.
2. The case labels should end with a colon.
3. The case labels should have constants or constant expressions.

4. The case label should be on an integral type, such as integer or character.
5. The case label should not be a floating point number.
6. The switch case should have a default label.
7. The default label is optional.
8. The default may be placed anywhere in the switch.
9. The break statement should take control out of the switch.
10.   A break statement may be shared by at least two cases.
11.   Nesting, which is basically using a switch within a switch, can be used.
12.   Relational operators should not be used in a switch statement.
13.   Macro identifiers can be used as switch case labels.
14.   The const variable can be used in a switch case statement.
15.   An empty switch case can be used.

In order to make these rules clearer, you should consider the following examples for every rule:

Rule 1: The case labels should be unique.

Example:

int id = 3;

switch (id)

{

case 1:

```
printf ("C Language");

break;

case 2:

printf ("C++ Language");

break;

case 3:

printf ("Java Language");

break;

default:

printf ("No student found");

break;

}
```

Rule 2: The case labels should end with a colon.

Example:

```
case 1:

printf ("C Language");

break;
```

Rule 3: The case labels should have constants or constant expressions.

Example:

case 1+1:

case 67:

case 'A':

Keep in mind that variables should not be used. Therefore, you cannot use the following:

case num2:

case var:

Rule 4: The case label should be on an integral type, such as integer or character.

Example:

case 20:

case 30 + 30:

case 'B':

case 'b':

Rule 5: The case label should not be a floating point number.

Example:

You cannot use a decimal value, such as:

case 2.5:

Rule 6: The switch case should have a default label.

Example:

switch (roll)

{

case 1:

printf ("C Language");

break;

case 2:

printf ("C++ Language");

break;

case 3:

printf ("Java Language");

break;

default:

printf ("Default Version 1");

break;

default:

printf ("Default Version 2");

break;

}

Rule 7: The default label is optional.

Example:

switch (roll)

{

case 1:

printf ("C Language");

break;

case 2:

printf ("C++ Language");

break;

case 3:

printf ("Java Language");

break;

}

Keep in mind that your program will still produce the same output even if you do not include default labels.

Rule 8: The default may be placed anywhere in the switch.

Example:

```
switch (roll)

{

case 1:

printf ("C Language");

break;

case 2:

printf ("C++ Language");

break;

default:

printf ("No student found");

break;

case 3:

printf ("Java Language");
```

break;

}

Rule 9: The break statement should take control out of the switch.

Rule 10: A break statement may be shared by at least two cases.

Example:

switch (beta)

{

case 'a':

case 'A':

printf ("Letter A");

break;

case 'b':

case 'B':

printf ("Letter B");

break;

}

Rule 11: Nesting, which is basically using a switch within a switch, can be used.

Example:

```
switch (beta)

{

case 'a':

case 'A':

printf ("Letter A");

break;

case 'b':

case 'B':

switch (beta)

{

}

break;

}
```

Rule 12: Relational operators should not be used in a switch statement.

Example:

```
switch (num)

{

case >14:

printf ("Number > 14");

break;

case =14:

printf ("Number = 14");

break;

case <14:

printf ("Number < 14");

break;

}
```

Remember that you cannot use relational operators as switch labels.

Rule 13: Macro identifiers can be used as switch case labels.

Example:

```
#define MAX 1

switch (num)
```

{

case MAX:

printf ("Number = 1");

break;

}

Rule 14: The const variable can be used in a switch case statement.

Example:

int const var = 1;

switch (num)

{

case var:

printf ("Number = 1");

break;

}

Flow Diagram

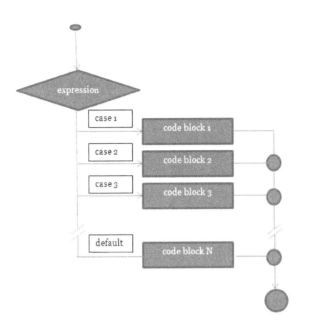

Example:

#include <stdio.h>

int main ( )

{

/* local variable definition */

char grade = 'B';

switch (grade)

```
{
case 'A' :
printf ( "Excellent !\n" );
break;
case 'B' :
case 'C' :
printf ( "Well done\n" );
break;
case 'D' :
printf ( :You passed\n" );
break;
case 'F' :
printf ( "Better try again\n" );
break;
default :
printf ( "Invalid grade\n" );
}
printf ( "Your grade is %c\n", grade );
return o;
```

}

Once the above code is executed, the following output is shown:

Well done

Your grade is B

Nested Switch Statements

If you are wondering whether or not it is possible to use a switch in an outer switch statement sequence, the answer is yes. You can include a switch in the statement sequence without encountering any conflicts even though the case constants of the outer and inner switch have common values.

Syntax

This is the general syntax for a nested switch:

switch (ch 1)

{

case 'A':

printf ("This A is part of the outer switch");

switch (ch 2)

```c
{
case 'A':
printf ("This A is part of the inner switch" );
break;
case 'B':
/* case code */
}
break;
case 'B':
/* case code */
}
```

Example:

```c
#include <stdio.h>
int main ( )
{
/* local variable definition */
int a = 100;
int b = 200;
```

```
switch (a)
{
case 100:
printf ("This is part of the outer switch\n", a );
switch (b)
{
case 200:
printf ("This is part of the inner switch\n", a );
}
}
printf ("The exact value of a is : %d\n", a );
printf ("The exact value of b is : %d\n", b);
return 0;
}
```

Once the above code is executed, the following output is shown:

This is part of the outer switch

This is part of the inner switch

The exact value of a is : 100

The exact value of b is : 200

The ?: Operator

You can use the ?: operator as a replacement for an if else statement. Its general form is as follows:

Exp1 ? Exp2 : Exp3;

Exp1, Exp2, and Exp3 are types of expressions. Make sure that you take note of the placement of the colon in the statement. Keep in mind that the value of ? is determined as such:

Exp1 is first assessed. If it is proven to be true, Exp2 is assessed next and it serves as the current expression value. On the other hand, if Exp1 is proven to be false, then Exp3 is assessed next and its value serves as the current expression value.

Chapter 8 C Loops

In case you have to execute a block of code a few times, you should execute the statements sequentially. This means that you have to execute the first statement in a function first, and then the second, and so on.

A loop statement allows you to execute a statement or a number of statements several times. The following is the general form of a loop statement:

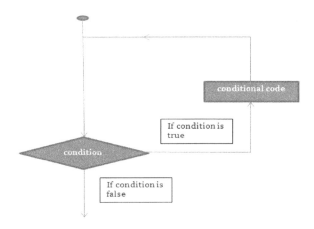

The Different Types of Loops

While Loop

The while loop repeatedly executes a particular statement if the given condition is true.

Syntax

The general syntax of a while loop is as follows:

while (condition)

{

statement(s);

}

You can use a single statement or a block of statements in a while loop. Also, you can give a condition of any expression, but non-zero values are considered true. As long as the condition is true, the loop continues to iterate. Once the condition becomes false, the program control passes to the line that immediately follows the loop.

Flow Diagram

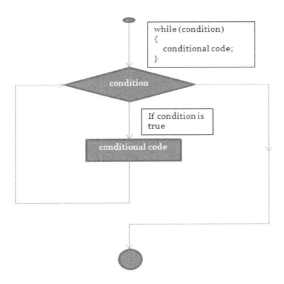

If the condition of the while loop is tested and found to be false, then the first statement after the while loop is executed while the loop body is skipped.

Example:

#include <stdio.h>

int main ( )

{

/* local variable definition */

int x = 10;

/* while loop execution */

```
while ( x < 20)

{

printf ("The value of x: %d\n", x);

x++;

}

return 0;

}
```

Once the above code has been executed, the following output is shown:

The value of x: 10

The value of x: 11

The value of x: 12

The value of x: 13

The value of x: 14

The value of x: 15

The value of x: 16

The value of x: 17

The value of x: 18

The value of x: 19

For Loop

The for loop is used to repeat a certain block of codes for a certain number of times.

Syntax

This is the general syntax for a for loop:

```
for ( init; condition; increment )
{
statement(s);
}
```

Flow Diagram

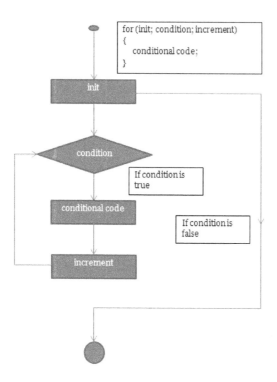

The Flow of Control in a For Loop

First, the init is executed to enable you to initialize and declare loop control variables. As long as you use a semicolon, there is no need for you to place a statement here.

Then, the condition is evaluated. If it is proven to be true, then the loop is executed. Otherwise, the flow of control moves on to the next statement.

After the body of the for loop is executed, the flow of control moves back to the increment. The increment statement allows you to update your loop control variables. You can leave it blank if you want for as long as you use a semicolon after your condition.

Finally, the condition is re-evaluated. If it is found to be true, then the loop executes and the entire process is repeated. When the condition becomes false, the for loop terminates.

Example:

```
#include <stdio.h>

int main ( )

{

/* for loop execution */

for ( int x = 10; x < 20; x = x + 1)

{

printf ("The value of x: %d\n", x);

}

return 0;

}
```

Once the above code is executed, the following output is shown:

The value of x : 10

The value of x : 11

The value of x : 12

The value of x : 13

The value of x : 14

The value of x : 15

The value of x : 16

The value of x : 17

The value of x : 18

The value of x : 19

Different Ways of Using For Loop

If you want to perform a certain action multiple times, you can use loop control statements. You can write for loop using the following:

1. Single Statement Inside For Loop

   Example:
   for (i = 0; i < 5; i++)
   printf ("Programming");

2. Multiple Statements Inside For Loop

Example:
```c
for (i = 0; i < 5; i++)
{
printf ("First Statement");
printf ("Second Statement");
printf ("Third Statement");

if (condition)
{

}
}
```

3. No Statement Inside For Loop

Example:
```c
for (i = 0; i < 5; i++)
{

}
```

4. Semicolon at the End of For Loop

Example:
```c
for (i = 0; i < 5; i++);
```

5. Multiple Initialization Statement Inside For Loop

Example:
```
for (i = 0; j = 0; i < 5; i++)
{
statement 1;
statement 2;
statement 3;
}
```

6. Missing Increment/Decrement Statement

Example:
```
for (i = 0; i < 5; )
{
statement 1;
statement 2;
statement 3;
i++
}
```

7. Missing Initialization in For Loop

Example:
```
i = 0;
for ( ; i < 5; i++ )
{
statement 1;
statement 2;
statement 3;
}
```

8. Infinite For Loop

Example:
```
i = 0;
for ( ; ; )
{
statement 1;
statement 2;
statement 3;

if (breaking condition)
break;

i++;
}
```

Do While Loop

Just like the while loop, the do while loop is also used for looping. The loop condition is tested at the end of the loop and the loop is executed at least once. However, unlike the while loop, the do while loop is rarely used by most programmers.

Syntax

The general syntax for the do while loop is as follows:

Do

```
{

statement(s);

}

while (condition);
```

As you can see from the above example, the conditional expression is found at the end of the loop. Hence, the statement(s) in the loop is/are executed once before the condition is tested. If the condition is found to be true, the flow of control moves back up to do and the statement(s) is/are executed once more. The process continues to repeat until the condition is found to be false.

Flow Diagram

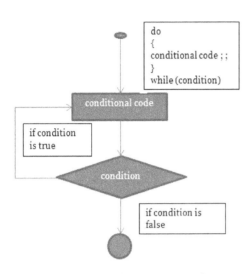

Example:

```
#include <stdio.h>
int main ( )
{
/* local variable definition */
int x = 10;
/* do loop execution */
do
{
```

```c
printf ("The value of x: %d\n, x);
x = x + 1;
}
while (x < 20);
return 0;
}
```

Once the above code is executed, the following output is shown:

The value of x: 10

The value of x: 11

The value of x: 12

The value of x: 13

The value of x: 14

The value of x: 15

The value of x: 16

The value of x: 17

The value of x: 18

The value of x: 19

Nested Loops

The usage of one loop inside another is allowed in the C programming language. This is what nested loops are all about.

Syntax

This is the general syntax for nested loops:

```
for ( init; condition; increment )
{
for ( init; condition; increment )
{
statement(s);
{
statement(s);
}
```

This is the general syntax for a nested do while loop:

```
do
{
statement(s);
do
{
statement(s);
}
```

```
while (condition);
}
while (condition);
```

Take note that when it comes to loop nesting, you can place whatever type of loop you want inside any other type of loop. For instance, you can put a while loop inside a for loop and vice versa.

Example:

```
#include <stdio.h>
int main ( )
{
/* local variable definition */
int a, b;
for (a = 2; a < 100; a++)
{
for (b = 2; b <= (a/b); b++)
if (! (a % b)) break; // if a factor is found, it is not a prime number
if (b > (a/b)) printf ("%d is a prime number\n", a);
}
return 0;
```

```
}
```

Once the above code is executed, the following output is shown:

2 is a prime number

3 is a prime number

5 is a prime number

7 is a prime number

11 is a prime number

13 is a prime number

17 is a prime number

19 is a prime number

23 is a prime number

29 is a prime number

31 is a prime number

37 is a prime number

41 is a prime number

43 is a prime number

47 is a prime number

53 is a prime number

59 is a prime number

61 is a prime number

67 is a prime number

71 is a prime number

73 is a prime number

79 is a prime number

83 is a prime number

89 is a prime number

97 is a prime number

Break Statement

The break statement contains two main functions:

1. If the break statement is found in a loop, then the loop is terminated immediately and the program control goes to the next statement that follows the loop.

2. The break statement can be used for case termination in a switch statement.

If you are running nested loops, the break statement stops the running of the innermost loop and begins executing the code found after it.

Syntax

This is the general syntax of a break statement:

break;

Flow Diagram

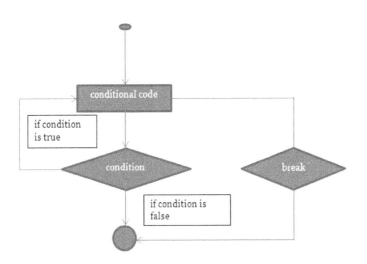

Example:

```
#include <stdio.h>
int main ( )
{
/* local variable definition */
int y = 10;
/* while loop execution */
while (y < 20)
{
```

```
printf ("The value of y: %d\n", y);
y++;
if (y > 15)
{
/* terminate the loop using break statement */
break;
}
}
return 0;
}
```

Once the above code is executed, the following output is shown:

The value of y: 10

The value of y: 11

The value of y: 12

The value of y: 13

The value of y: 14

The value of y: 15

Continue Statement

The continue statement is similar to the break statement, except that it does not force termination but rather continues to force the next loop iteration to occur while it skips any codes in between.

If you are using a for loop, the continue statement causes the increments and conditional tests of the loop to execute. If you are using a do while or while loop, the continue statement causes the program control to move on to the conditional tests.

Syntax

The following is the general syntax for a continue statement:

continue;

Flow Diagram

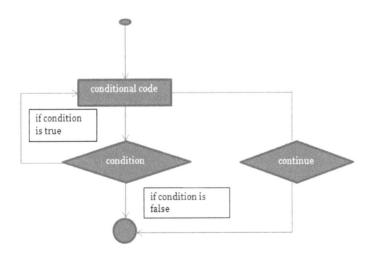

Example:

```
#include <stdio.h>
int main ( )
{
/* local variable definition */
int y = 10;
/* do loop execution */
do
{
if ( y == 15 )
{
/* skip the iteration */
y = y + 1;
continue
}
printf ("The value of y: %d\n", y);
y++;
}
while ( y < 20 );
return 0;
}
```

Once the above code is compiled and executed, the following output is shown:

The value of y: 10

The value of y: 11

The value of y: 12

The value of y: 13

The value of y: 14

The value of y: 16

The value of y: 17

The value of y: 18

The value of y: 19

Goto Statement

The goto statement causes the control to jump to the corresponding label that is mentioned with goto. However, goto is rarely used for applications and level prorgamming because it can be quite confusing, complex, and less readable. It also makes the control of the program difficult to trace. Likewise, it tends to make debugging and testing hard to do.

Syntax

This is the general syntax of a goto statement:

goto label;

..

..

label: statement;

Flow Diagram

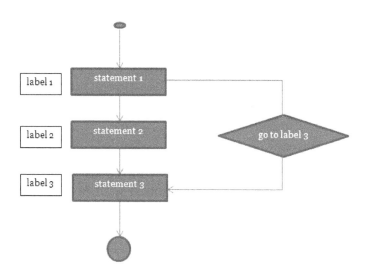

Example:

#include <stdio.h>

```c
int main ( )
{
/* local variable definition */
int w = 10;
/* do loop execution */
LOOP:do
{
if ( w == 15)
{
/* skip the iteration */
w = w + 1;
goto LOOP;
}
printf ("The value of w: %d\n", w);
w++;
}
while ( w < 20 );
return 0;
}
```

Once the above code is executed, the following output is shown:

The value of w: 10

The value of w: 11

The value of w: 12

The value of w: 13

The value of w: 14

The value of w: 16

The value of w: 17

The value of w: 18

The value of w: 19

The Infinite Loop

It can be said that a loop is infinite if its condition never becomes false. Traditionally, the for loop is used for this purpose. However, since the expressions found in the for loop are not required, you can leave out the condition to create an endless loop.

```c
#include <stdio.h>
int main ( )
for ( ; ; )
{
printf ("This is an endless loop.\n");
}
```

```
return 0;

}
```

If the condition is not present, then it is presumed to be true. It is alright to use an increment expression or initialization, but you can also use the for (; ;) construct if you want to indicate an endless loop. Also, you can press the Ctrl + C keys to terminate an endless loop.

Chapter 9 Type Casting and Error Handling

Type Casting

One way to change a variable from a certain type of data to another is to use type casting. For instance, if you wish to store a long value into an integer, you can type cast long to int. Also, you can turn a value from a certain type to another by making use of the cast operator (type_name) expression.

The following is an example of a floating-point operation dividing two integer variables as a result of the usage of a cast operator:

```
#include <stdio.h>

main ( )

{

int sum = 17, count = 5;

double mean;

mean = (double) sum / count;

printf ("The mean value is : %f\n", mean);

}
```

Once this code is executed, the following output is shown:

The mean value is : 3.400000

You should take note that in this case, the cast operator precedes the division process. Hence, the sum value is converted first into a type double. Eventually, it gets divided by count and yields to a double value.

Integer Promotion

The process wherein the integer values that are smaller than unsigned int or int are turned into unsigned int or int is called integer promotion. Consider the following example:

```
#include <stdio.h>
main ( )
{
int i = 17;
char c = 'c'; /* The ASCII value is 99 */
int sum;
sum = i + c;
printf ("The value of sum : %d\n", sum);
}
```

Once the above code is executed, the following output is shown:

The value of sum : 116

The value of the sum is 116 because the compiler does integer promotion and converts the value of c to ASCII before it performs the actual addition process.

Usual Arithmetic Convertion

Usual arithmetic convertions are performed to cast values in a common type. The compiler does integer promotion. If the operands still have different types, they are converted into the highest type in this hierarchy:

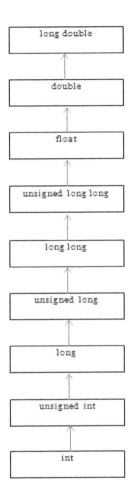

The usual arithmetic conversions are neither done for the logical operators || and && nor the assignment operators. Consider the example below:

```
#include <stdio.h>
main ( )
{
int i = 17;
char c = 'c'; /* The ASCII value is 99 */
float sum;
sum = i + c;
printf ("The value of sum : %f\n", sum);
}
```

Once the above code is executed, the following output is shown:

The value of sum : 116.000000

The first c is converted into an integer. However, because the final value is a double, the usual arithmetic conversion is applied and the compiler converts i and c into a float, adds them, and gets a float result.

Error Handling

In the C programming language, direct support for error handling is not provided. Nonetheless, it gives access at lower levels in the form of return values. Most C functions call return NULL or -1 in case of errors and set an error code errno.

As a programmer, you should make it a habit to set errno to o during the time of your program initialization. Remember that the value o indicates the absence of error in the program. In addition, see to it that you always check if a divisor is zero. If it is, you may encounter a runtime error.

Errno, Perror ( ), and Strerror ( )

Perror ( ) and strerror ( ) are functions that display text messages associated with errno. Perror ( ) displays the string that you pass onto it, a colon, a space, and the text of your current errno value. Strerror ( ), on the other hand, returns a pointer to the text of your current errno value.

Conclusion

Thank you again for purchasing this book!

I hope this book was able to help you to understand the complex terms and language used in C. this programming method can put off a lot of users because of its seemingly complexity. However, with the right basic knowledge, soon, you will be programming more complex things with C.

The next step is to start executing these examples. Reading and understanding this book is not enough, although this will push you into the right direction. Execution will cement the knowledge and give you the skill and deeper understanding of C.

Finally, if you enjoyed this book, please take the time to share your thoughts and post a review on Amazon. We do our best to reach out to readers and provide the best value we can. Your positive review will help us achieve that. It'd be greatly appreciated!

Thank you and good luck!

Check Out My Other Books

Below you'll find some of my other popular books that are popular on Amazon and Kindle as well. Simply click on the links below to check them out. Alternatively, you can visit my author page on Amazon to see other work done by me.

C Programming Success in a Day

Android Programming in a Day

C ++ Programming Success in a Day

Python Programming in a Day

PHP Programming Professional Made Easy

CSS Programming Professional Made Easy

Windows 8 Tips for Beginners

If the links do not work, for whatever reason, you can simply search for these titles on the Amazon website to find them.

www.ingramcontent.com/pod-product-compliance
Lightning Source LLC
Chambersburg PA
CBHW070838070326
40690CB00009B/1607